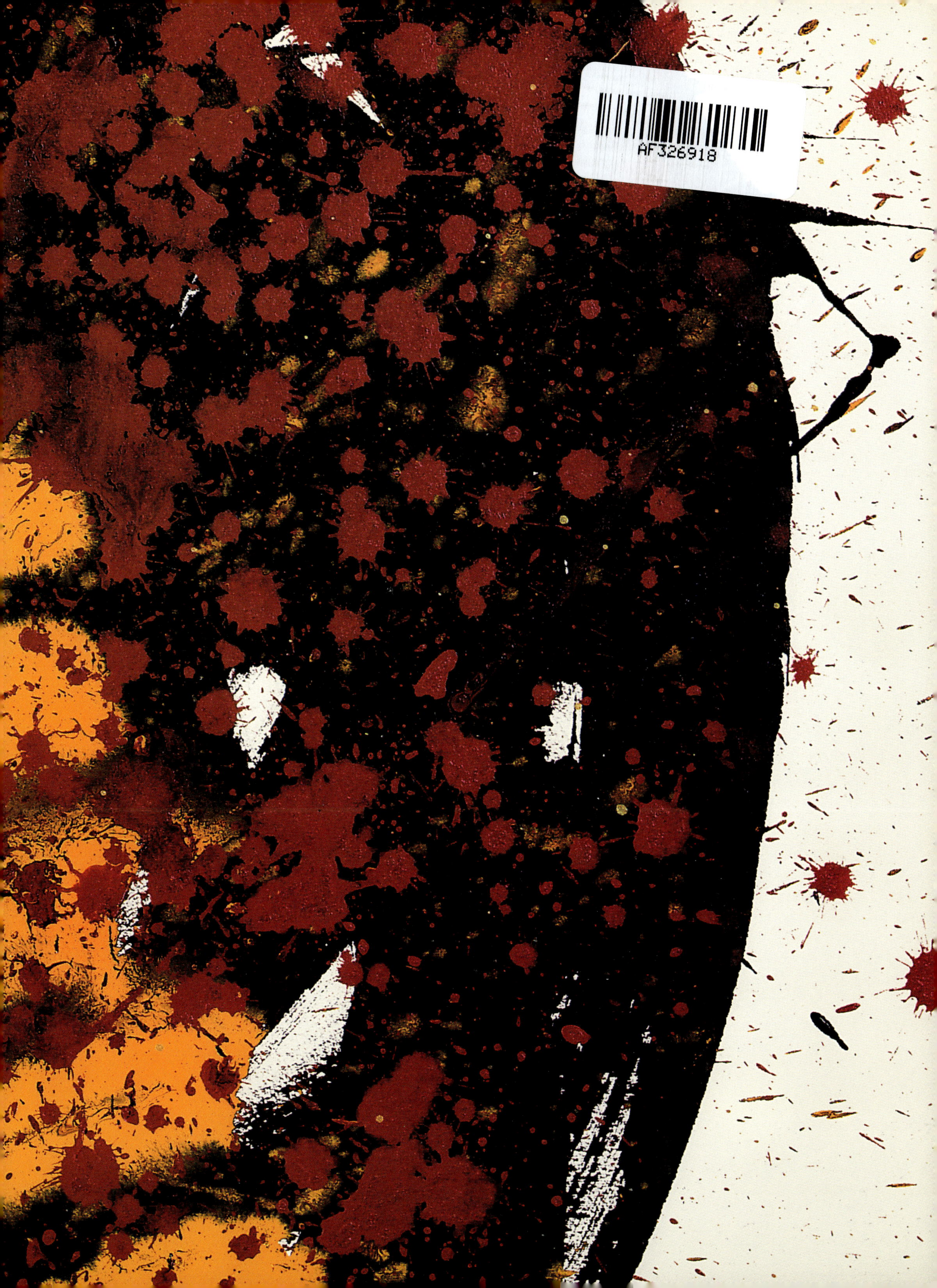
AF326918

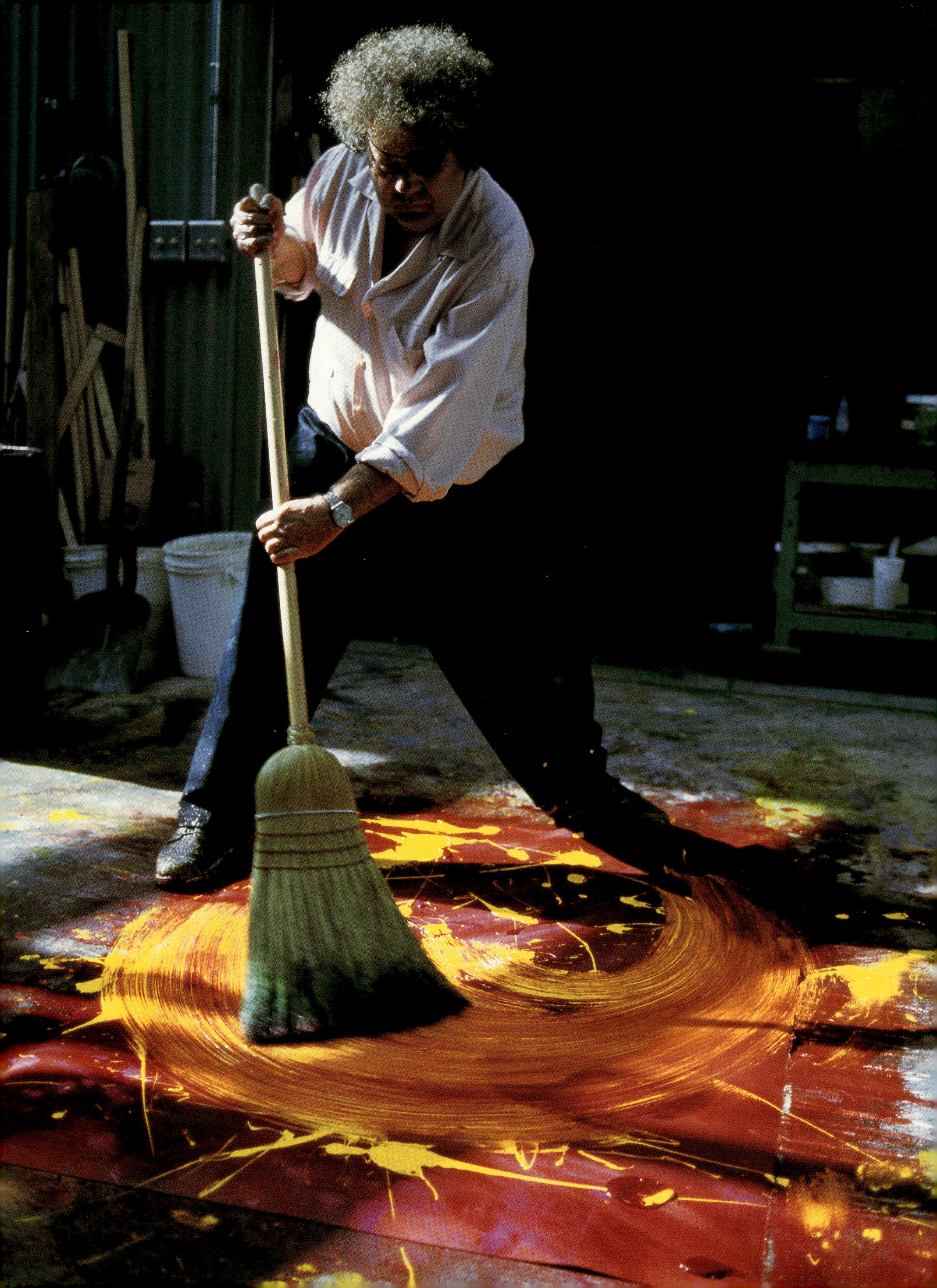

CHIHULY IN AUSTRALIA

GLASS AND WORKS ON PAPER

GEOFFREY EDWARDS

Cover:
Red Over Yellow Venetian with One Coil
1991
37 x 14 x 14 in.

Inside front cover:
Sisters Drawing (detail)
1991
Mixed mediums on paper
41 x 29 in.

Inside back cover:
Hawaii Drawing (detail)
1992
Mixed mediums on paper
41 x 29 in.

Page 2:
Dale Chihuly drawing in Boathouse hot shop

CHIHULY IN AUSTRALIA:
GLASS AND WORKS ON PAPER

Geoffrey Edwards, Curator of Sculpture and Glass,
National Gallery of Victoria, Melbourne.

Printed in the U.S.A.

ISBN 0-9608382-1-X

Publication edited by Diana Johnson and coordinated
by Karen S. Chambers assisted by Laura Brunsman

Designed by W. Joseph Gagnon with Ted Cotrotsos

Printed and bound by R-4 Typographers, Tacoma, Washington, U.S.A.

Generous support from Air New Zealand Cargo helped make this
exhibition possible.

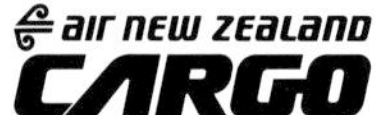

Photo credits:
Claire Garoutte: Cover, 8, 9, 10, 12, 13, 15, 16, 17, 18, 21
Bradley Goda: Inside back cover
Russell Johnson: 2
Terry Rishel: 20
Roger Schreiber: 11, 14, 19
Mike Seidl: Inside front cover, 1, 22, 23, 24, 25

Dale Chihuly in Australia

In spite of its venerable status as an art form, glass remains a medium of exquisite potential for the contemporary artist. Before the rise of the modern studio glass movement in the 1960s, connoisseurs of the subject harboured passions for specific episodes in glass history: for the bravura ornamentation of Murano glass made during the Renaissance in Venice, the handsome puritanism of 18th-century British lead crystal or the lyric naturalism of French turn-of-the-century pâte de verre.

Almost exclusively, these episodes would have been considered within the context of decorative or applied art. Glancing reference only was made to connections with other spheres of artistic endeavour. In effect, it has fallen to the contemporary artist in glass to forge crucial links with mainstream painting and sculpture and, on occasion, that curious hybrid 'installation' with its radical mix of sculpture, architecture and performance.

Much credit for this fresh perspective on glass is due to the American artist Dale Chihuly. His unmistakable shell-like forms with their rippling contours, luminous palette and finely veined or dappled patterns represent a seamless fusion of the great conventions of glassmaking with the formal rigour and challenge of contemporary painting and sculpture.

However, Chihuly's glass is so evocative of all manner of natural phenomena, from a butterfly wing to a parti-coloured strip of coral reef, that it seems absurd to describe it as abstract or even as expressionist in style. And yet, in spirit and fact, Chihuly's glass is aligned closely with the conceptual basis of contemporary sculpture, while many of his graphic emblems concur with developments in recent painting and printmaking. That said, Chihuly also reveals himself as an artist steeped in the heritage of centuries of glasshouse practice and is a natural heir to the celebrated Venetian tradition of gestural, hot-worked glass that, at its most progressive, is both virile and seductive.

It has been argued that in terms of technical and artistic innovation the comparatively recent emergence of the international studio movement marks a modern watershed in the long history of glass. Interestingly enough, this period of momentous development coincides with the dawn of a new millennium and so permits an intriguing comparison with the glass industry at the beginning of the first millennium.

At that time, Syrian glassmakers together with their counterparts
in Alexandria exercised a powerful monopoly of the thriving glass
industry throughout the Near East. The Syrians produced mostly
freely-blown wares, while the Alexandrians dominated trade in
decorative, kiln-worked glass. Accordingly, a typical Syrian flask in
clear glass was admired for its fluid and swelling form, limpid translu-
cency and delicate profile. By the same token, an Alexandrian mosaic
or *millefiore* cup was prized on account of its rich colour and intricate,
marbleized pattern.

Thus, we recognize the early emergence of two distinct interpreta-
tions of the medium that retain their currency and significance to the
present day. In essence, the first of these streams deals with the obvious
and fundamental use of glass as a ductile, visceral medium eminently
suited to the creation of organic or expressionist form. It is exemplified
by our delicately profiled Syrian vessel, but, more noticeably, by such
familiar products of Murano as the dashing, serpent-stemmed goblet
or fancy candelabrum studded with drifts of pert, furnace-worked
rosettes and buttressed by succulent tiers of pincered leaf tips.

In strict contrast, our second stream deals with the interpretation
of glass as a substitute for natural hard stones. Here the treatment of the
medium echoes the techniques of the lapidary, whose cutting and polish-
ing wheels create from simple blocks of stone, configurations notable for
their crisp angularity and swirling colour. Into this category comes
cameo glass, the *millefiore* and mosaic bowls already mentioned as the
stock-in-trade of Alexandrian craftsmen, and later Bohemian developments in cut and engraved decoration, together with Friedrich
Egermann's lush imitation of semi-precious stones known as 'Lithyalin.'

With the glass of Dale Chihuly, we observe a masterly synthesis
of qualities from both of these streams. Invariably, the gestural or
Venetian tradition is acknowledged as the signal influence on Chihuly's
metier. To a very real degree, however, the artist's work incorporates
aspects of the dual streams of the Syrian and Alexandrian models.
This is not to suggest that Chihuly's glass is fraught with any sense
of dichotomy in attitude, for the reality of the situation is quite the

reverse. In Chihuly's single forms and multiple compositions alike, these streams are galvanised into a poignant harmony in which reference to the natural world at its most erotic appears inseparable from reference to ancient glass conventions at their most exotic.

As is the practice of many contemporary painters, sculptors and conceptual artists, Chihuly often works in series. Indeed, we look to the consecutive 'Sea Form,' 'Macchia' (meaning 'spotted'), 'Venetian' and 'Persian' series as testimony to the vigour and scope of the artist's imagination and his ability to plumb untapped potential within the sacrosanct glasshouse vernacular.

Given the scale of Chihuly's glass, it is not surprising to know that he works with a team of skilled glass artists. This preference arises from his early experience as a student in Venini's Murano glasshouse: the classic hierarchy of master-craftsman working in concert with skilled assistants who perform separate tasks in the blowing process.

This exhibition is the first opportunity for an Australian audience to appreciate the panoramic breadth of Chihuly's glass 'en masse.' The majority of Australians are coastal dwellers like Chihuly in his youth and are unlikely, therefore, to overlook the artist's repertoire of allusions to the ribbed, flecked and coiled forms of marine biology. Similarly, the exhibition affords first-hand exposure to Chihuly's mastery of saturated colour, the finely drawn volute and the juggling of yawning pods that swallow smaller, filigree treasures, while they are themselves captive of a quivering and ruffled outer mantle of the most splendid and mercurial kind. A collector or student of glass will catch glimpses here of a quotation from a classic Venini 'handkerchief' vase and there of a scallop-moulded flask of Roman origin.

Such is the artist's command of his subject, that his glass and drawings would seem to reflect the wisdom of an earlier observation by another aficionado of the Venetian style: John Ruskin, for whom 'fine art' was 'that in which the hand, the head and the heart of man go together.' How well Ruskin's words describe the method and philosophy that underlie the success and influence of glass by Dale Chihuly.

Geoffrey Edwards

Cadmium Orange Soft Cylinder with Yellow Lip Wrap
1992
16 x 18 x 13 in.

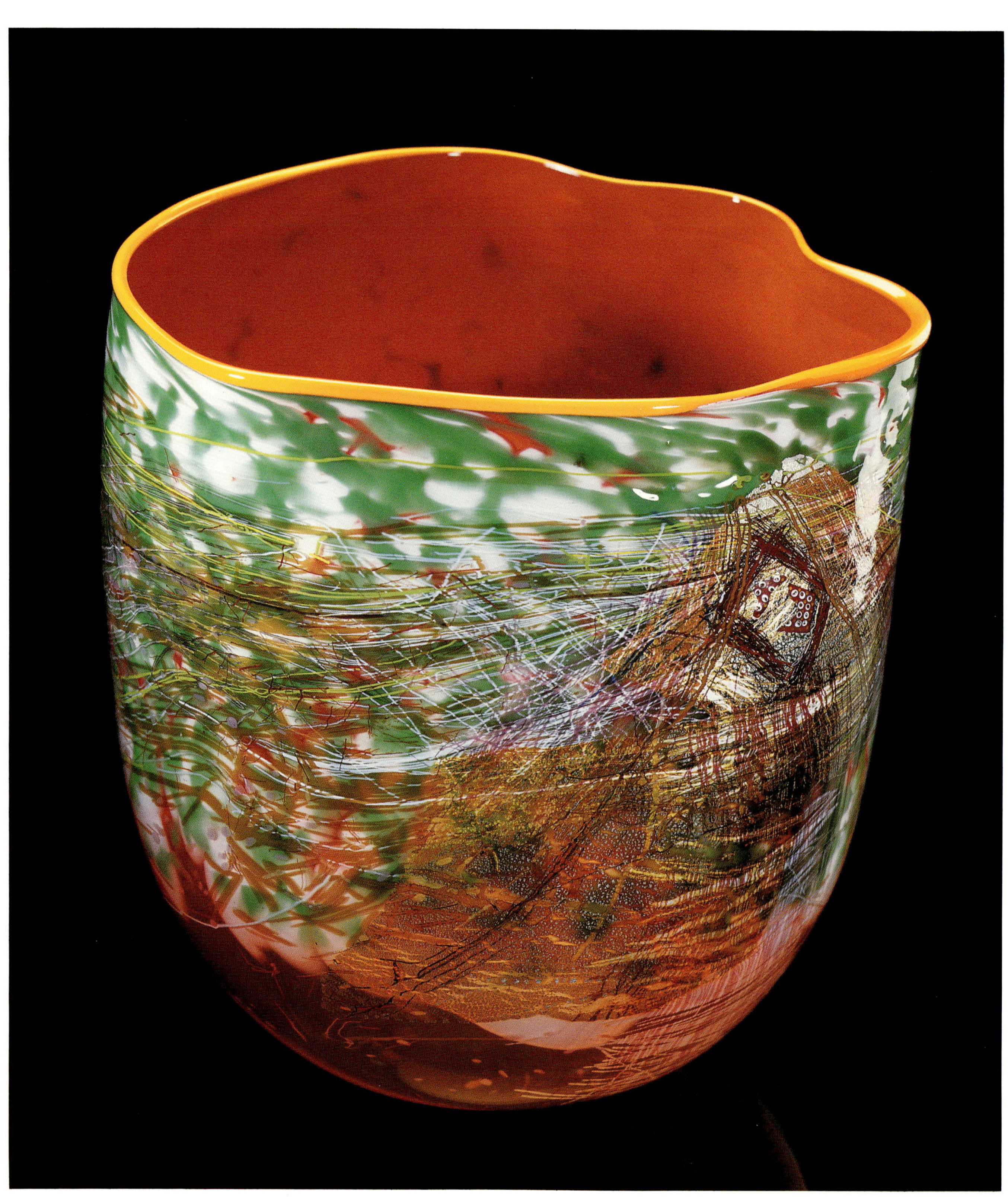

Translucent Yellow Basket Set with Black Lip Wraps
1992
16 x 20 x 17 in.

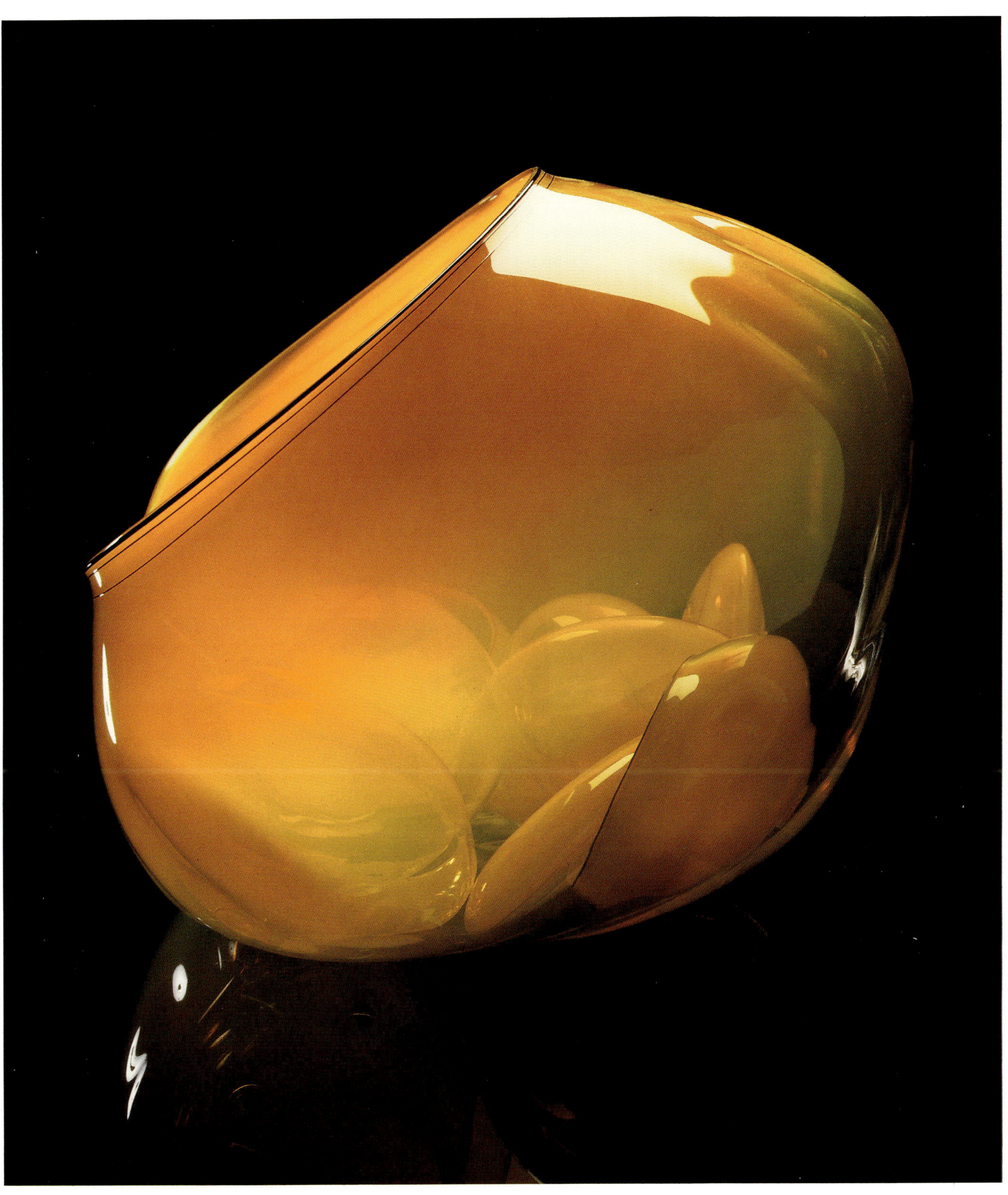

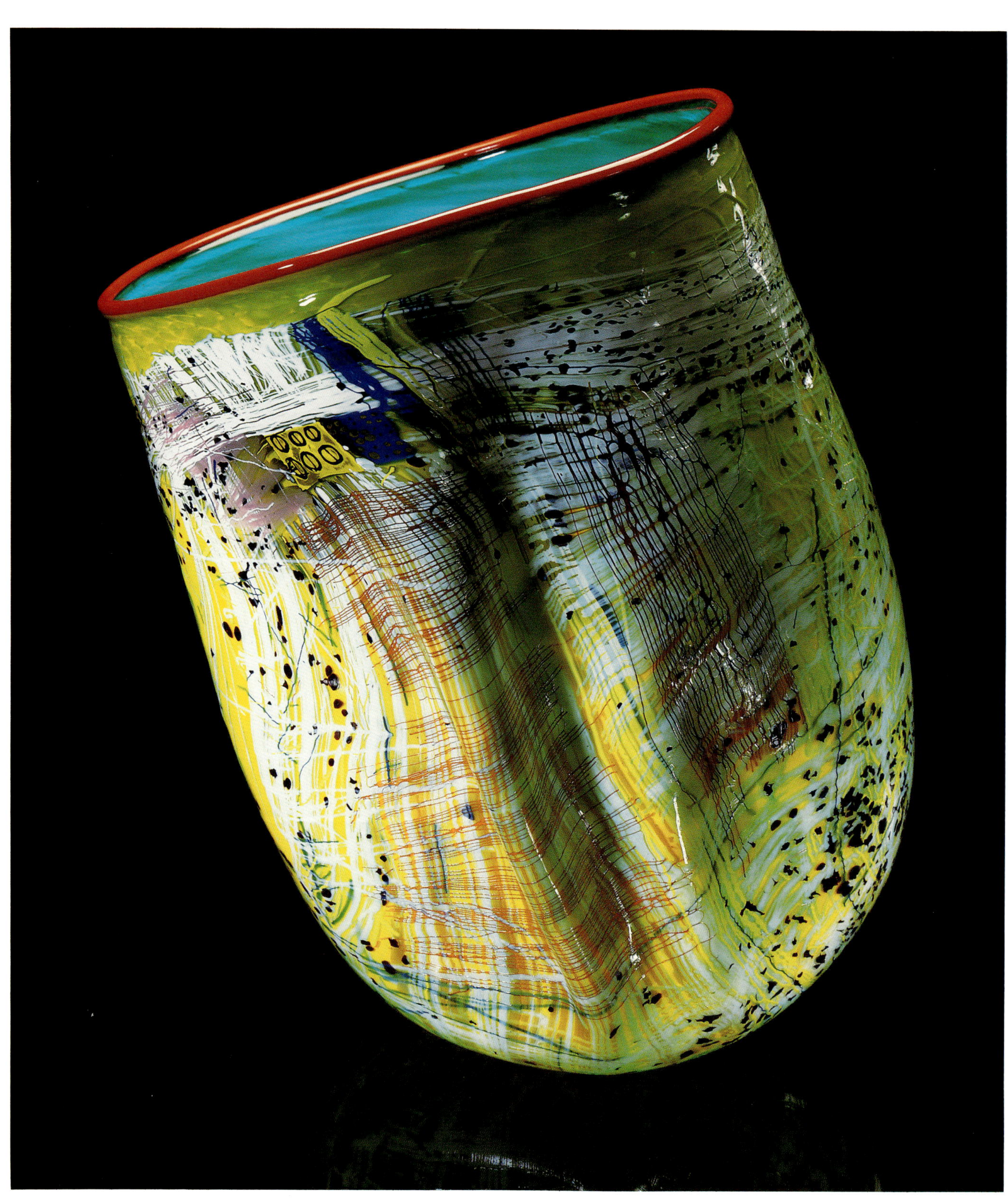

Pink Basket Set with White Lip Wraps
1990
14 x 34 x 31 in.

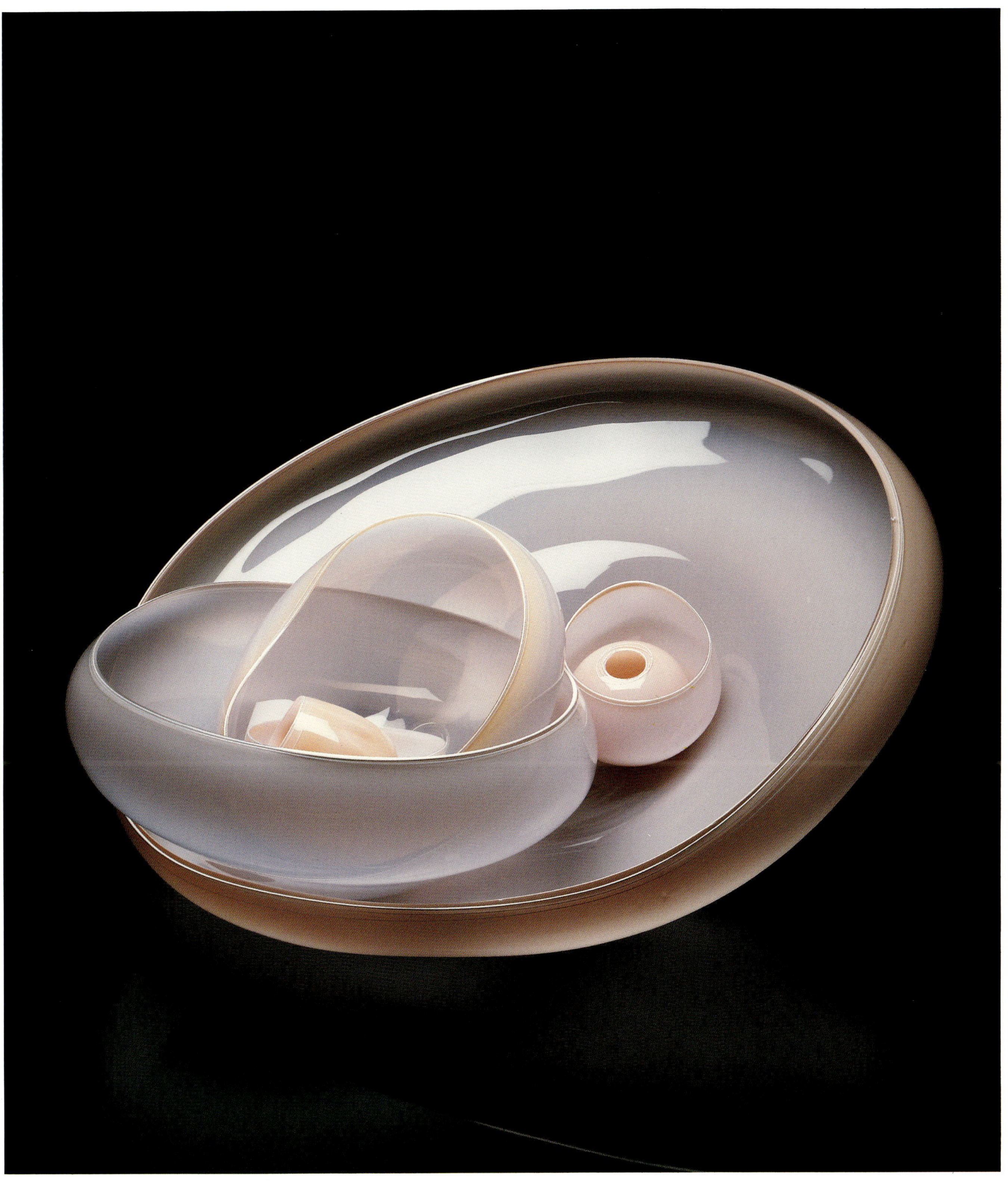

Winsor Green Macchia with Red Lip Wrap
1990
17 x 23 x 21 in.

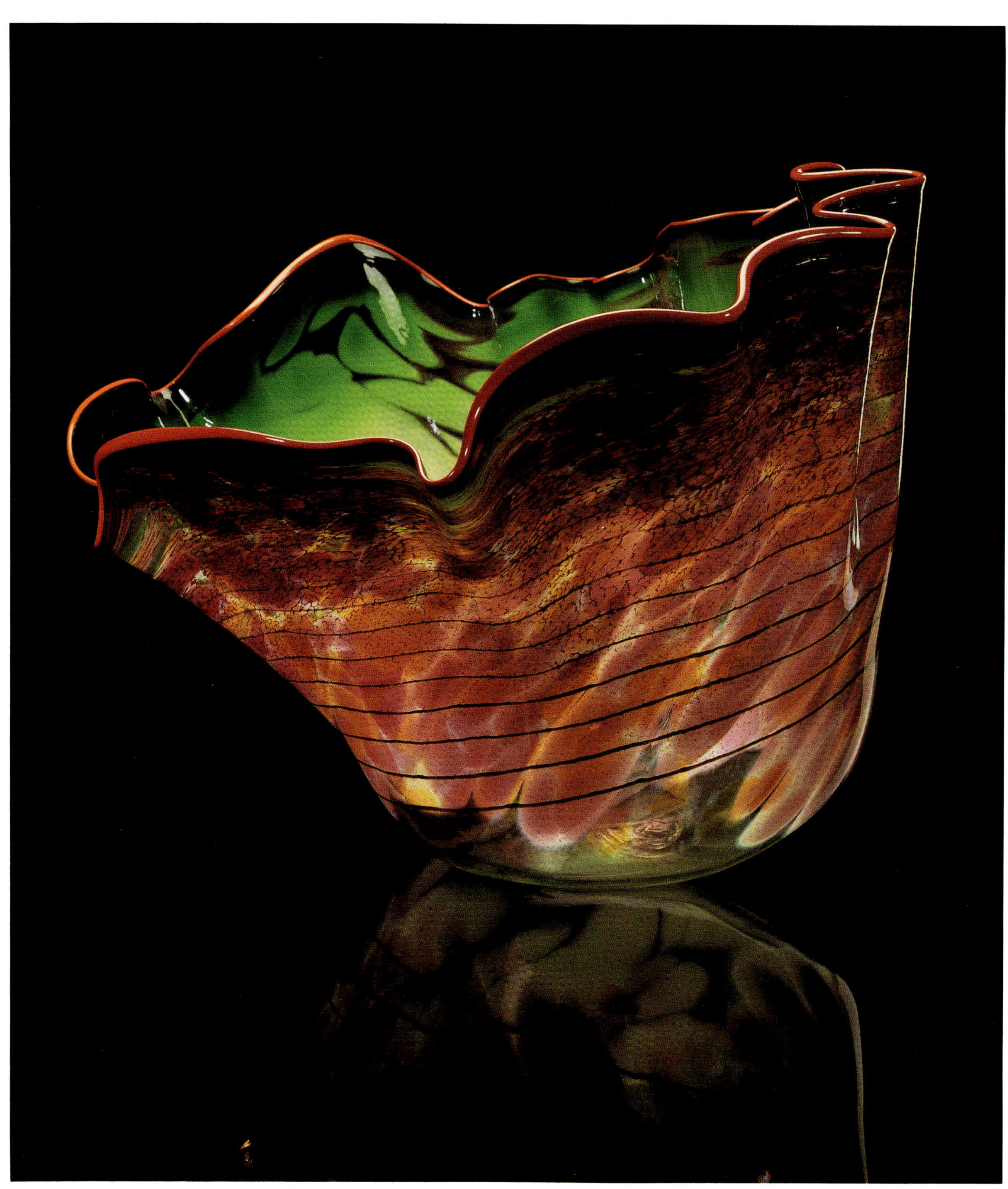

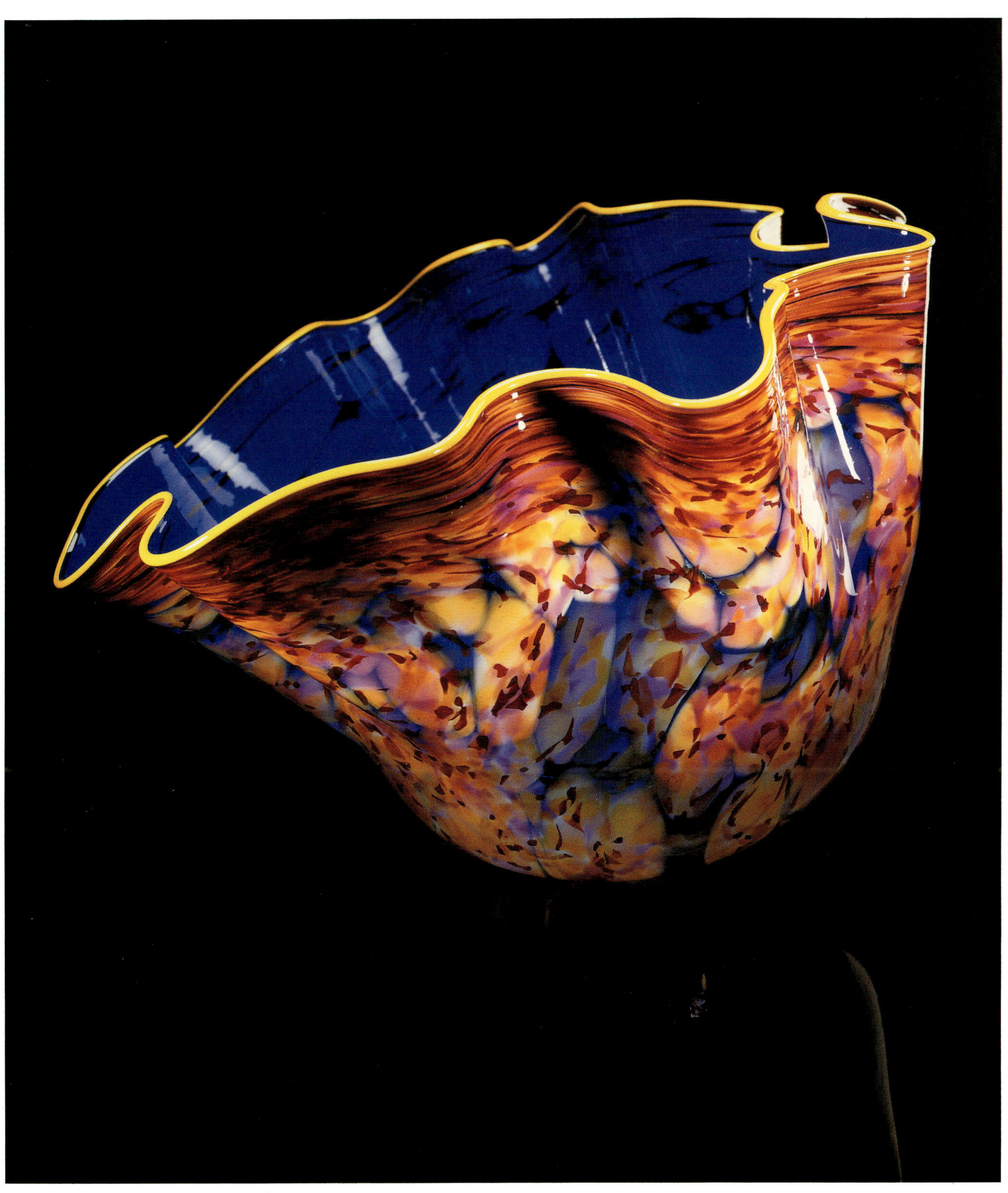

Violet Macchia Set with Teal Lip Wraps
1990
16 x 37 x 34 in.

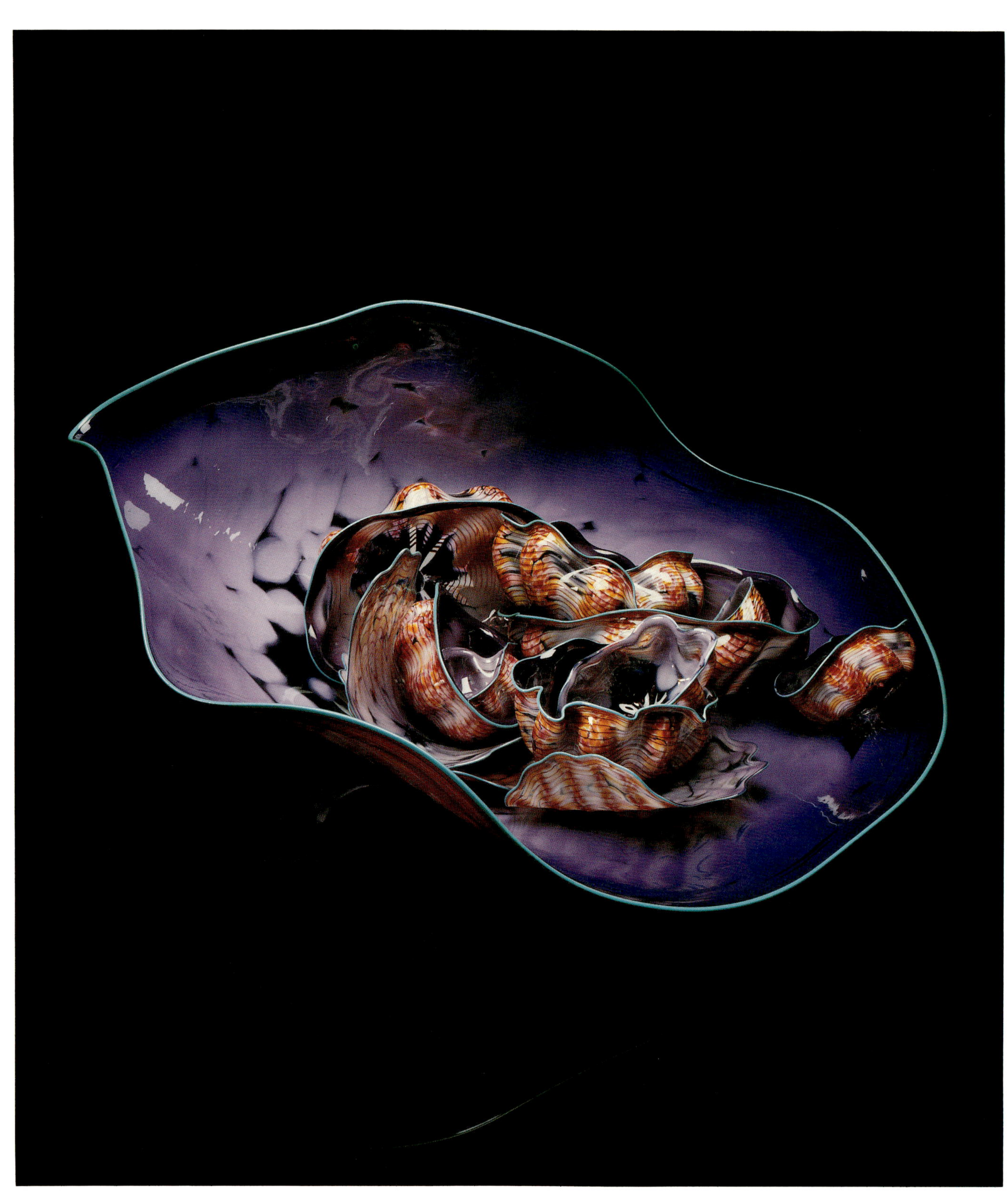

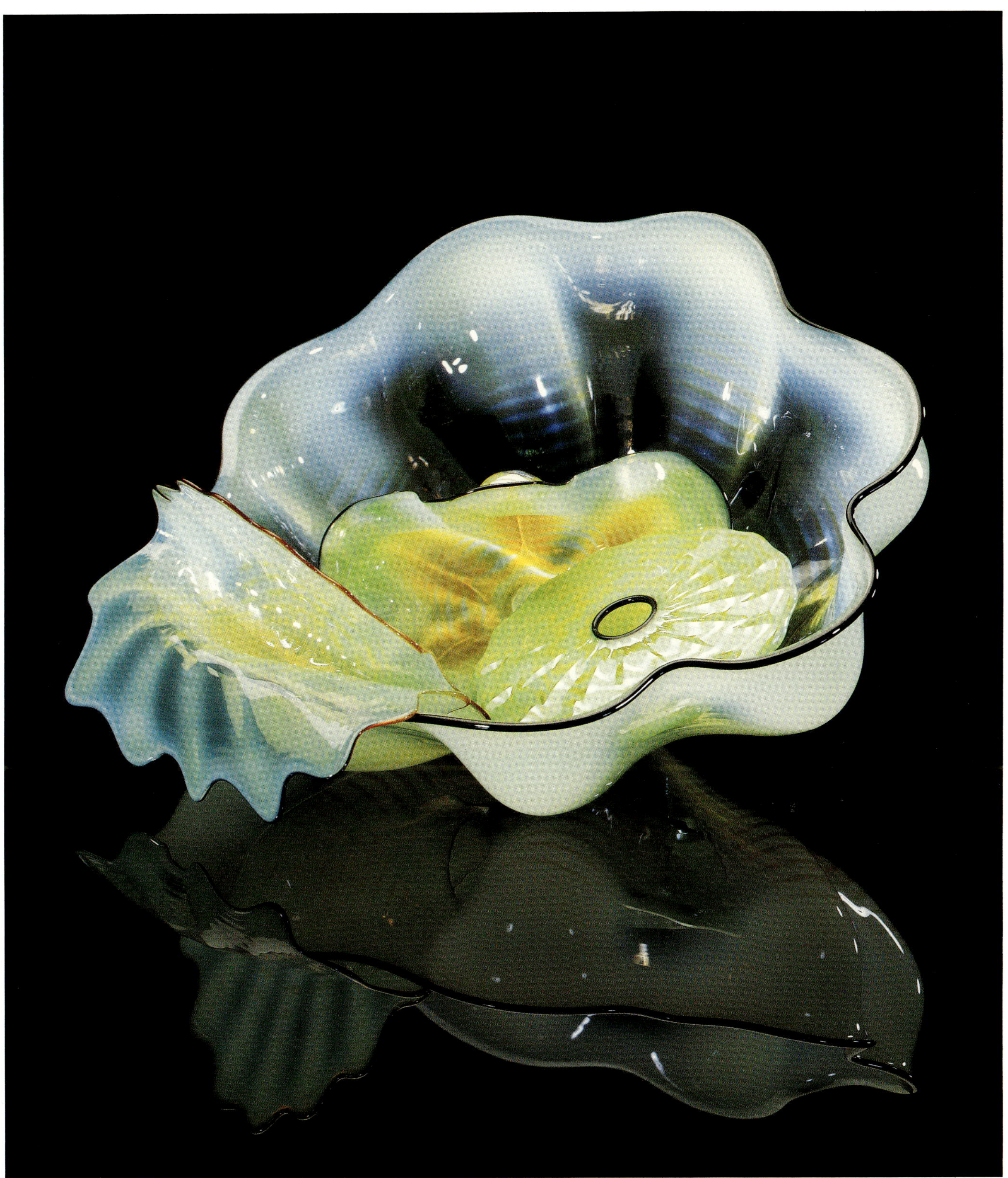

Silver and Oxblood Ikebana with Cadmium Yellow Leaf
1992
32 x 53 x 16 in.

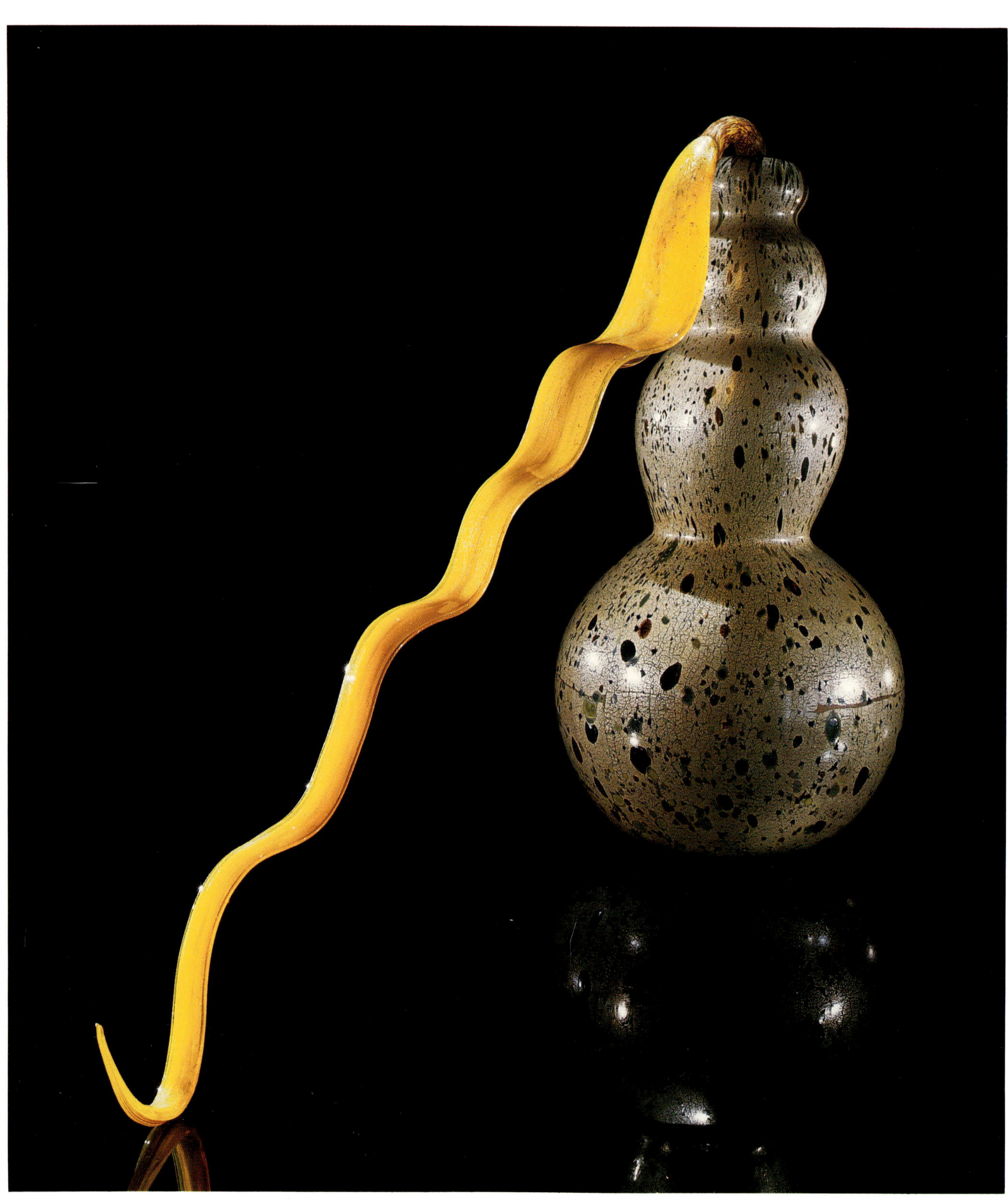

16

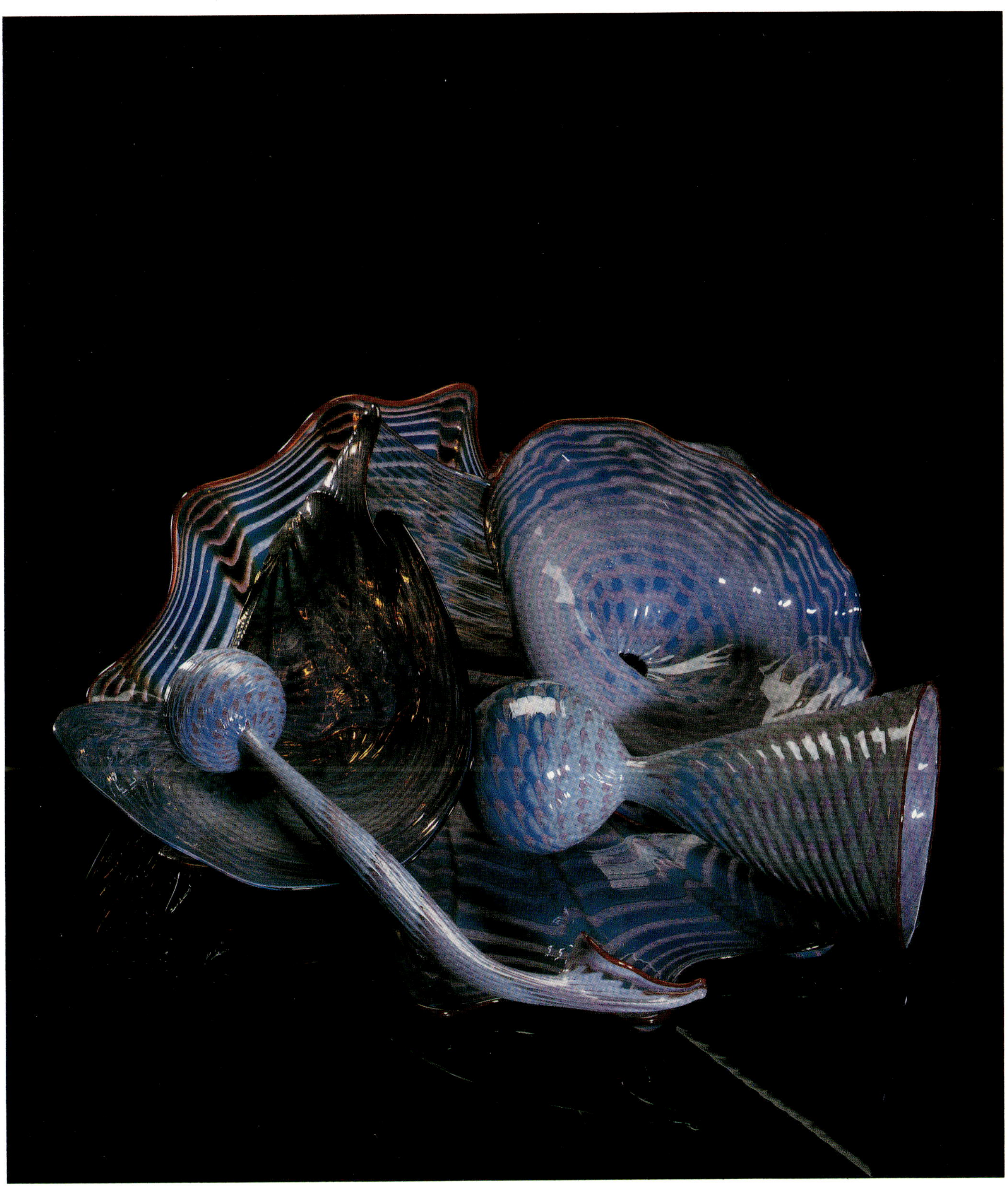

Lavender and Blue Wrapped Persian Set
1988
10 x 22 x 22 in.

Cadmium Yellow Persian
1992
13 x 27 x 16 in.

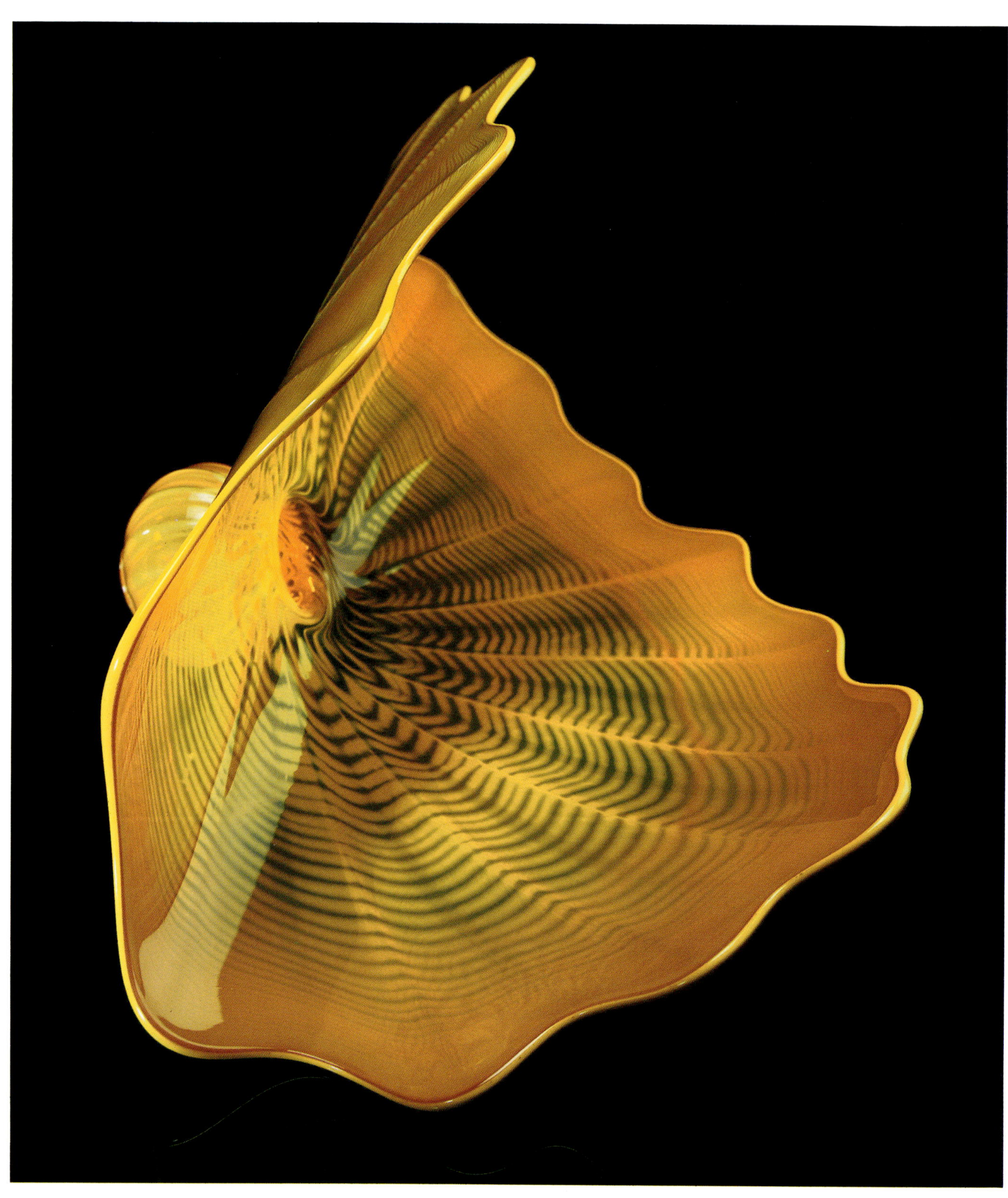

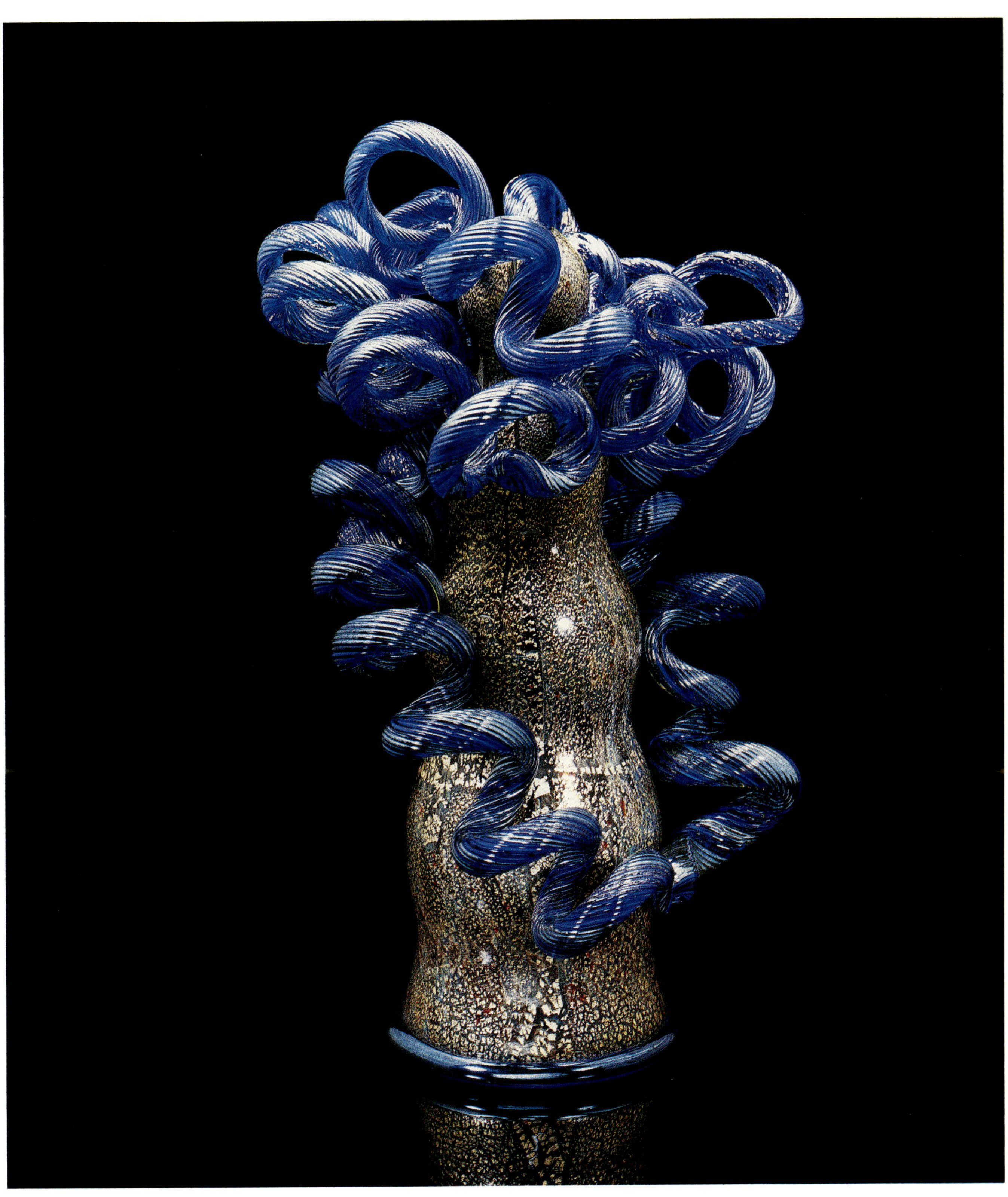

Indian Yellow Sea Form with Red Lip Wrap
1981
12 x 10 x 12 in.

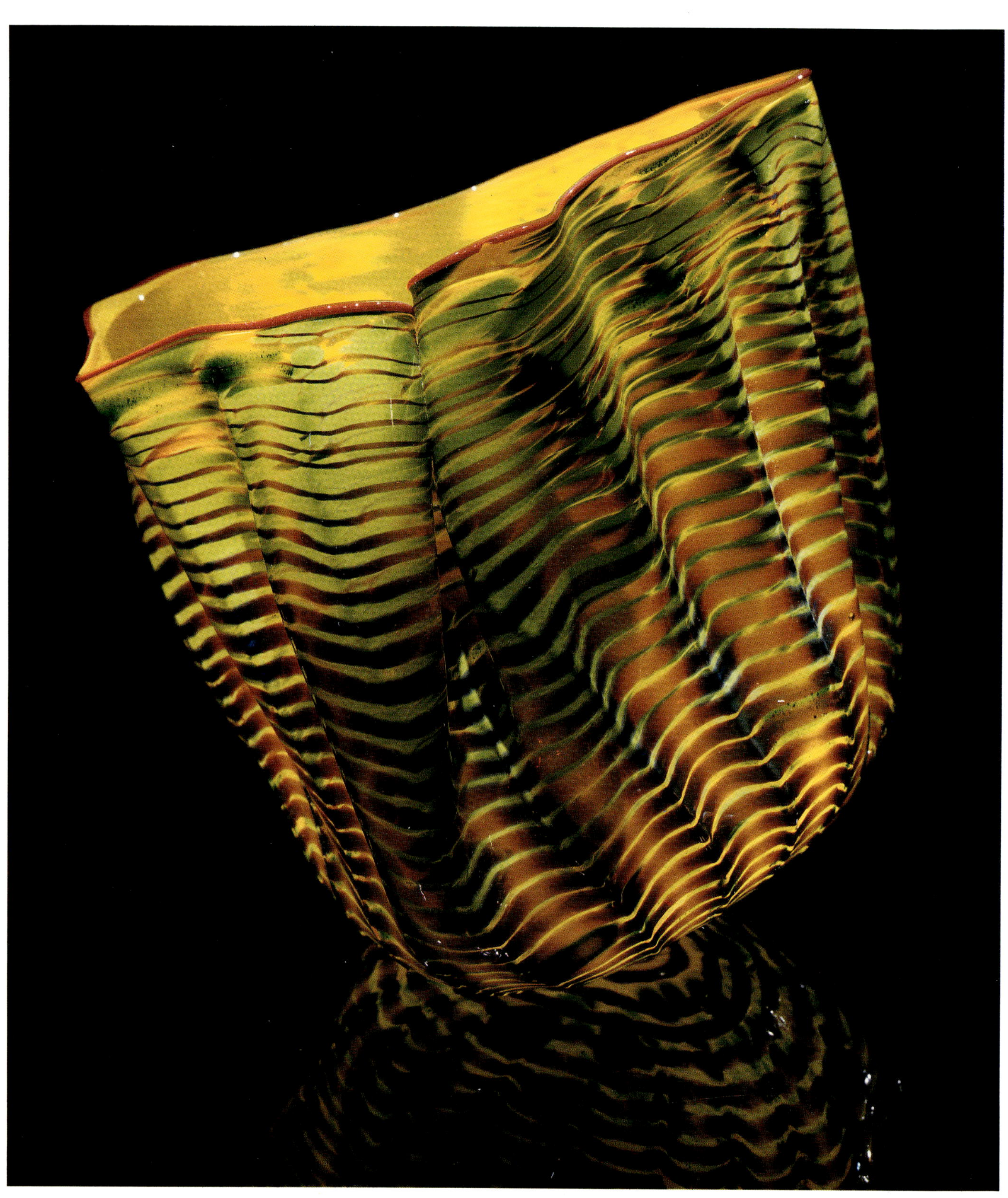

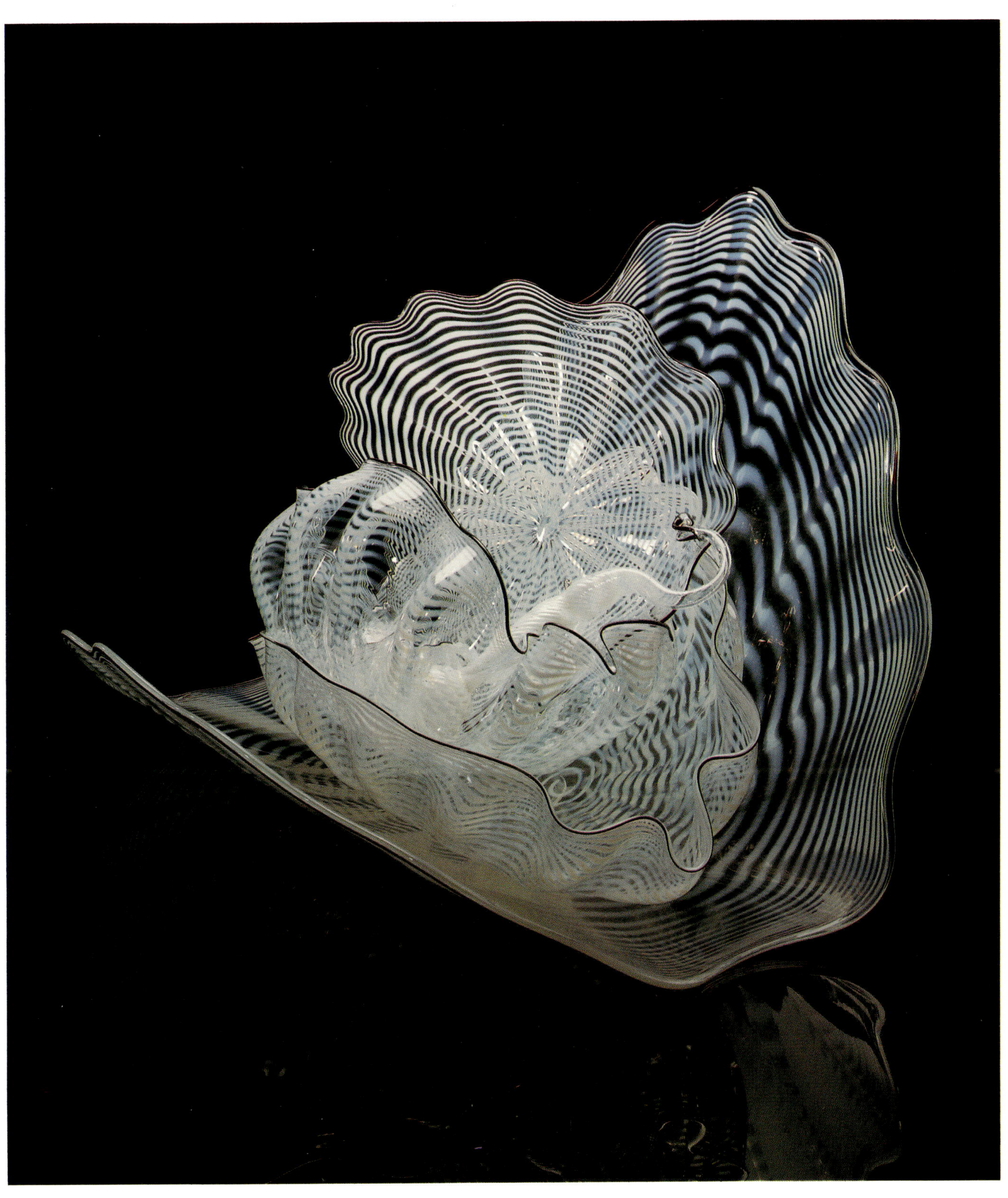

Venetian Drawing
1992
Mixed mediums on paper
30 x 22 in.

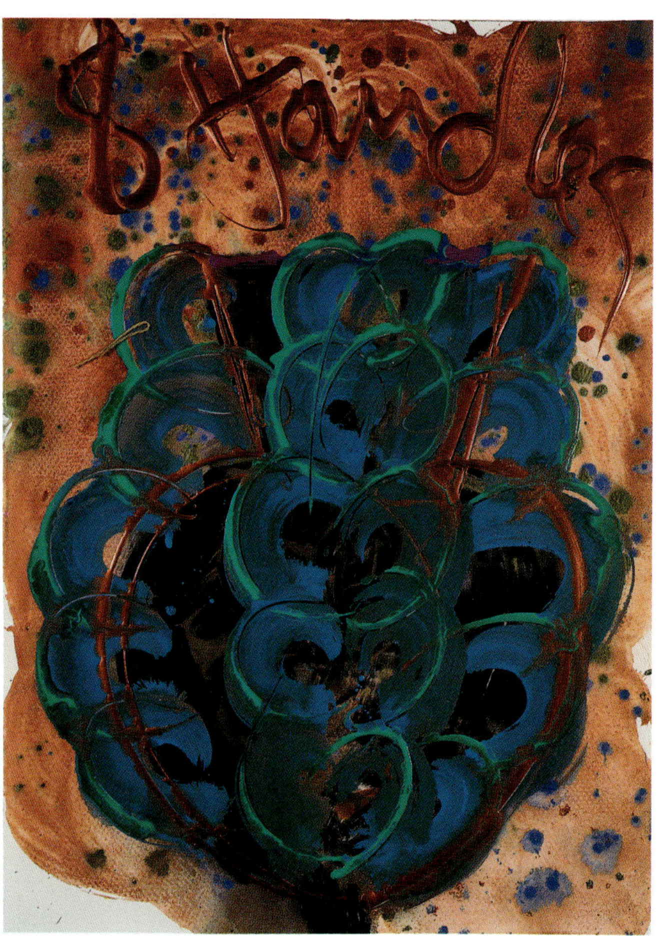

Venetian Drawing
1992
Mixed mediums on paper
30 x 22 in.

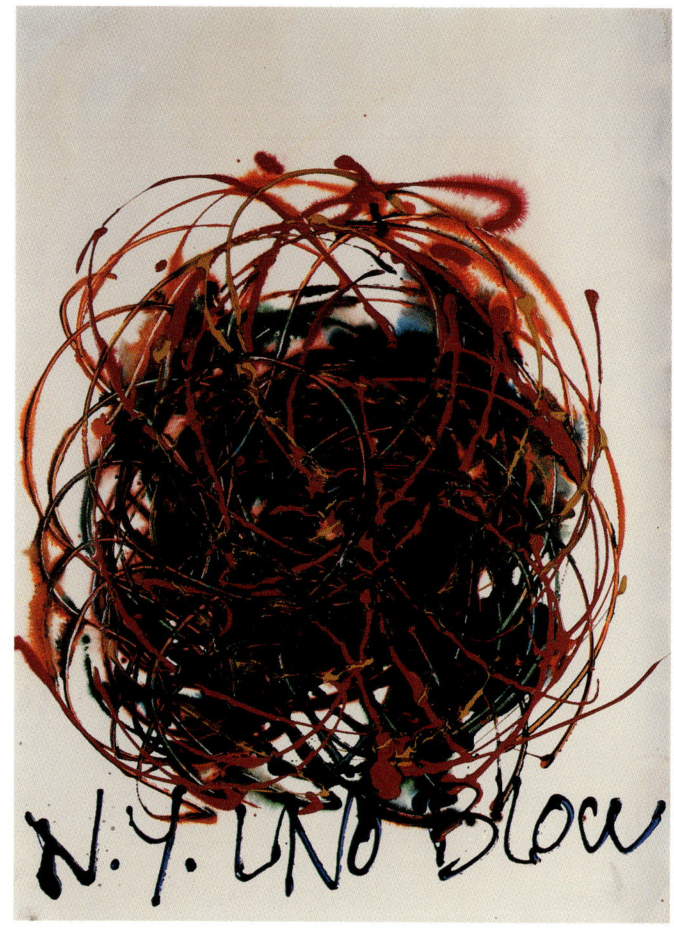

Venetian Drawing
1992
Mixed mediums on paper
30 x 22 in.

Venetian Drawing
1992
Mixed mediums on paper
30 x 22 in.

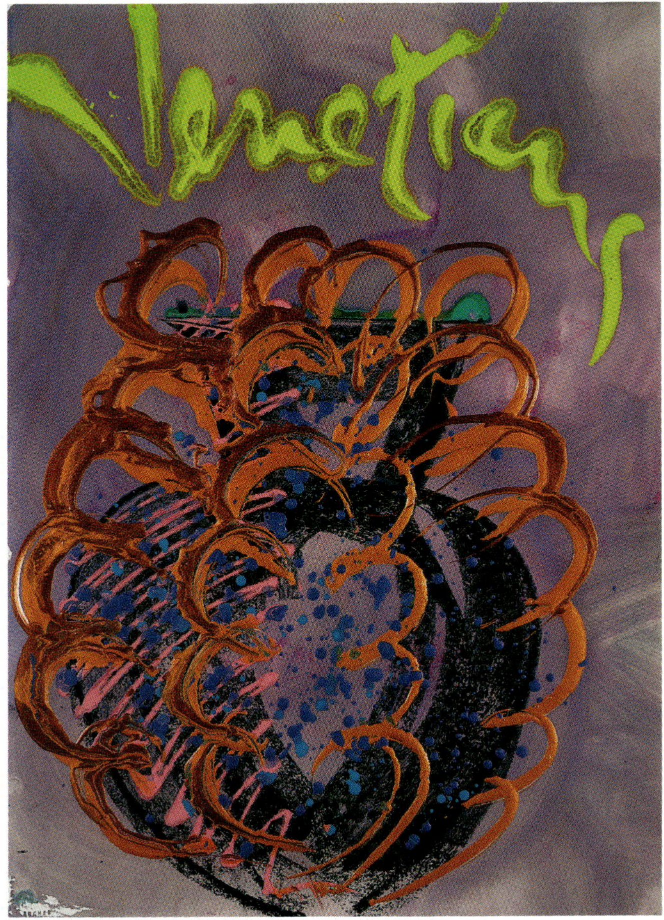

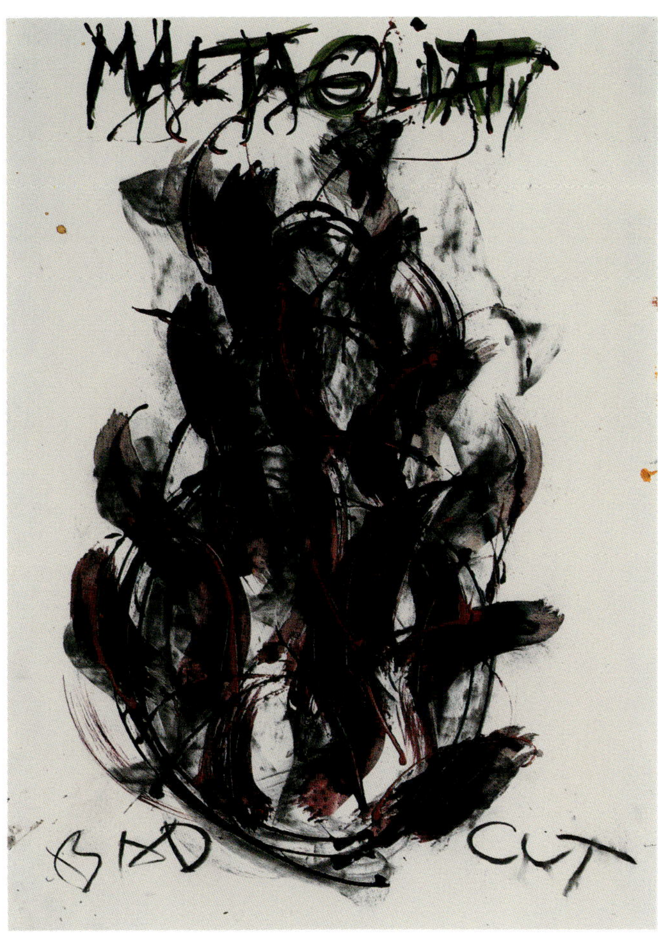

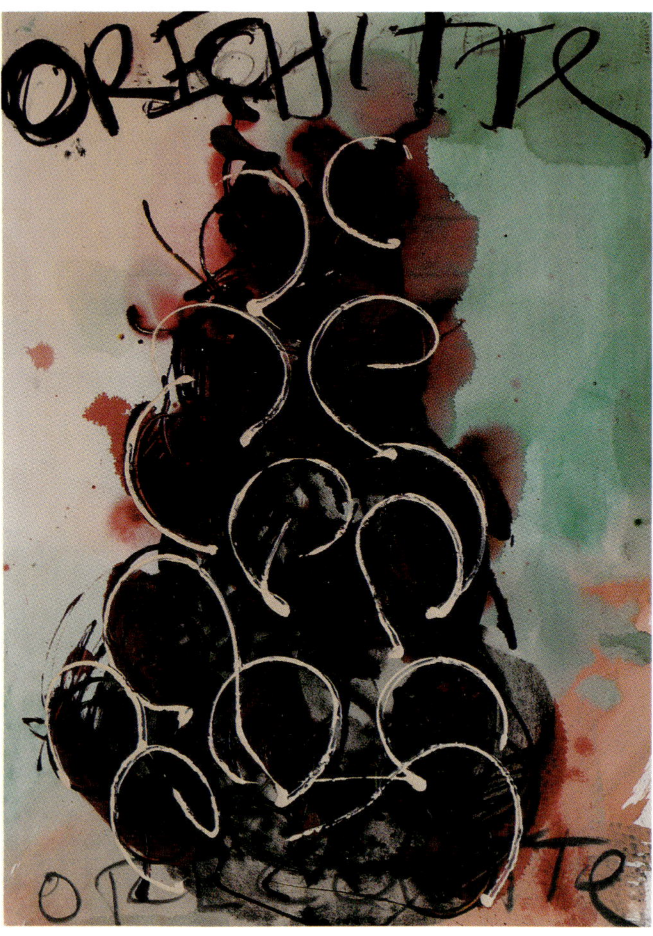

Venetian Drawing
1992
Mixed mediums on paper
30 x 22 in.

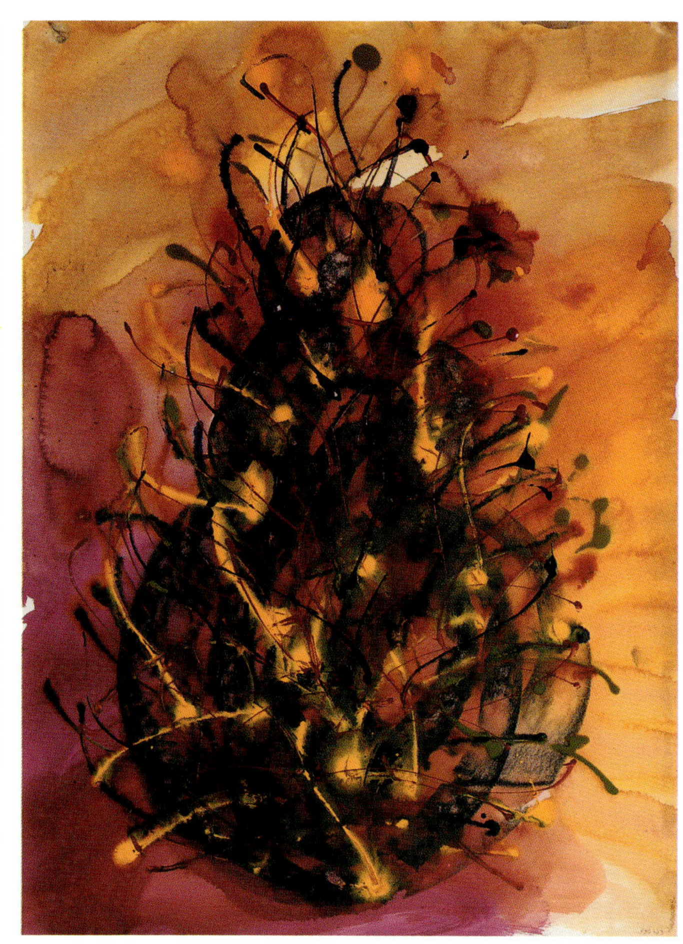

Venetian Drawing
1992
Mixed mediums on paper
30 x 22 in.

Venetian Drawing
1992
Mixed mediums on paper
30 x 22 in.

Venetian Drawing
1992
Mixed mediums on paper
30 x 22 in.

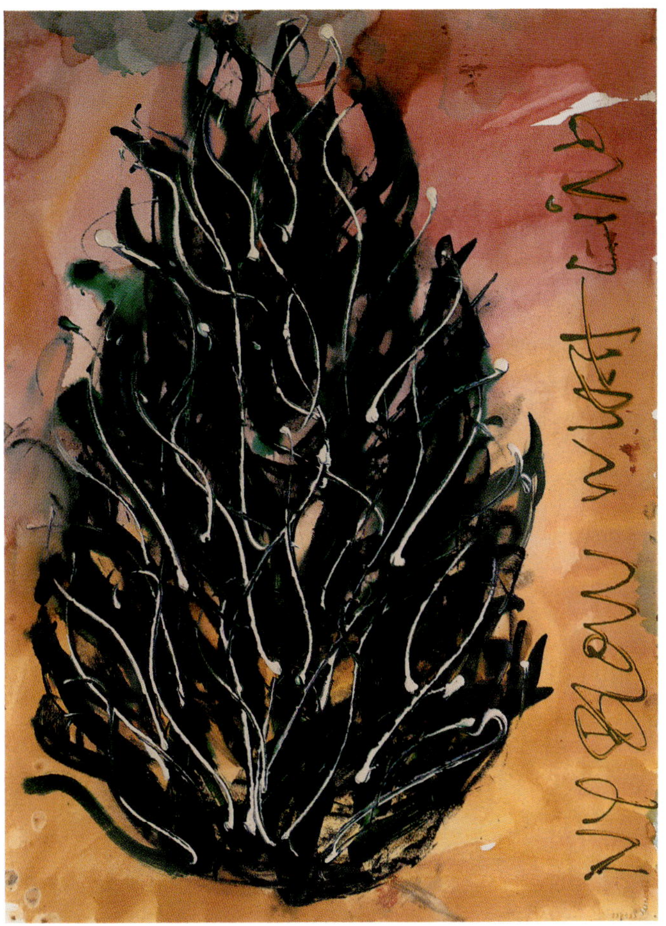

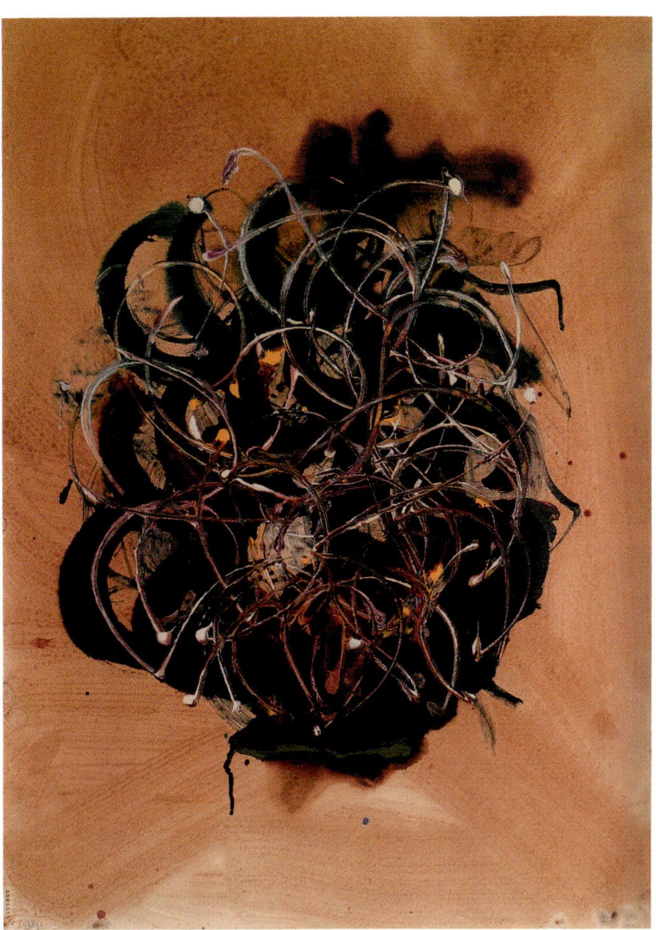

Dale Chihuly Chronology

1941 Born September 20, Tacoma, Washington, to Viola and George Chihuly, a union organiser.

1956 Older brother, George, killed in Navy Air Force training flight.

1957 Father dies.

1959 Enrolls in University of Puget Sound, Tacoma.

1960 Transfers to University of Washington, Seattle, in Interior Design.

1961-62 Learns to melt and fuse glass in his basement studio in south Seattle.

1962-63 Travels to Europe and Near East. In Israel works on a kibbutz.

1963 Re-enters University of Washington. In weaving classes with Doris Brockway begins incorporating glass into tapestries.

1964 Returns to Europe, visiting Leningrad and Ireland. Receives Seattle Weavers Guild Award.

1965 Awarded highest honors from the American Institute of Interior Designers (now the American Society of Interior Designers). Receives Bachelor of Arts in Interior Design, University of Washington. Experimenting on his own, blows glass for the first time.

1966 Works as commercial fisherman in Alaska earning money for graduate studies. On a full scholarship, enters University of Wisconsin, Madison, to study glass blowing with Harvey Littleton.

1967 Receives Master of Science from University of Wisconsin. Enrolls in Master of Fine Arts program at Rhode Island School of Design (R.I.S.D.). Meets Italo Scanga.

1968 Receives Master of Fine Arts from R.I.S.D. Awarded Tiffany Foundation Grant and Fulbright Fellowship to study glass in Venice, the first American glass blower to work on Murano.

1969 Continues at Venini. Makes pilgrimage to visit Erwin Eisch in Germany as well as Jaroslava Brychtova and Stanislav Libensky in Czechoslovakia. Returns to R.I.S.D. in the fall to establish glass department. Included in 'Objects U.S.A.' traveling exhibition circulated by the Smithsonian Institution, Washington, D.C.

1970 Meets James Carpenter at R.I.S.D. and begins four-year collaboration.

1971 With a grant from the Union of Independent Colleges of Art, starts Pilchuck Glass School in his home state of Washington with property donated by John Hauberg and Anne Gould Hauberg.

1972-73 Returns to Venice and blows glass. Works on glass architectural projects with Carpenter, including *Leaded Glass Door* for the Toledo Museum of Art. Included in traveling show 'American Glass Now' originated by the Corning Museum of Glass, New York.

1974 Experiments on new 'glass drawing pick-up techniques' at Pilchuck.

1975 Receives first of two National Endowment for the Arts grants. Develops 'Navajo Blanket Cylinder' series. Solo exhibition of 'Blanket Cylinders' at Utah Museum of Fine Arts, Salt Lake City, and Institute of American Indian Art, Santa Fe, New Mexico.

1976 Collaborates with Seaver Leslie on 'Irish' and 'Ulysses Cylinders,' with Flora Mace fabricating glass drawings. Travels with Leslie to Great Britain on lecture tour. Loses sight in left eye in serious automobile accident. Henry Geldzahler, curator of contemporary art at the Metropolitan Museum of Art, New York, purchases three 'Navajo Blanket Cylinders' for the permanent collection. Western Association of Art Museums circulates solo exhibition.

1977 Becomes head of R.I.S.D. sculpture department. Begins 'Pilchuck Basket' series at Pilchuck, inspired by seeing Northwest Coast Indian baskets at Washington State Historical Society, Tacoma.

1978	Meets William Morris, beginning an eight-year working relationship. Exhibition 'Baskets and Cylinders: Recent Work by Dale Chihuly' organised by Renwick Gallery, Smithsonian Institution, Washington, D.C.
1979	Relinquishes gaffer position when shoulder becomes dislocated in body surfing accident. Included in major American and European traveling exhibition, 'New Glass,' organised by the Corning Museum of Glass, New York.
1980	Becomes artist-in-residence at R.I.S.D. after resigning as head of Glass Department. Begins 'Sea Forms' series.
1981	Begins 'Macchia' series. Spends summer and fall at Pilchuck, preparing for solo show at Tacoma Art Museum, Washington.
1982	'Chihuly Glass' exhibition focusing on 'Sea Forms' opens at Tacoma Art Museum and travels through 1984 to five American museums.
1983	Sells 'Boathouse' studio in Rhode Island. Moves to Seattle to live and work.
1984	Honored as R.I.S.D. President's Fellow. Receives Visual Artist's Award from American Council for the Arts and first of three Washington State Governor's Art Awards. 'Chihuly: A Decade of Glass' opens at the Bellevue Art Museum, Washington, and travels to 13 museums in U.S. and Canada.
1985	Commissioned to do large architectural installations, including at The Seattle Aquarium as King County Arts Commission's Honors Award artist. Renovates Buffalo Shoe Building as studio in Seattle.
1986	Named Fellow of the American Craft Council. Receives honorary doctorates from the University of Puget Sound and R.I.S.D. and Governor's Art Award from Rhode Island. Returns to 'Cylinder' format with 'Soft Cylinders' series. Begins 'Persians' series working with gaffer Martin Blank. Kodansha International Ltd. publishes *Chihuly: Color, Glass and Form*. Traveling survey exhibition 'Dale Chihuly: objets de verre' organised by the Musée des Arts Décoratifs, Palais du Louvre, Paris.
1987	Completes *Rainbow Flower Frieze* installation at the Rockefeller Center, New York. Builds first glass blowing studio in Seattle at the Van De Kamp Building. 'Chihuly Collection' installed permanently at the Tacoma Art Museum.
1988	Begins 'Venetians' series with maestro Lino Tagliapietra. Receives honorary doctorate from California College of Arts and Crafts.
1989	Twin Palms publishes *Venetians: Dale Chihuly*. At Pilchuck works with Italian maestro Pino Signoretto, experimenting with additions of *putti* to 'Venetians.' Begins to experiment with Tagliapietra adding flower forms to 'Venetians' for the 'Ikebana' series.
1990	Renovates Seattle Pocock racing shell factory on Lake Union into new 'Boathouse,' incorporating glass blowing shop, studio and residence. 'Dale Chihuly: Japan 1990' presented by the Azabu Museum of Arts and Crafts of Tokyo.
1991	Completes major private and public architectural installations, including a Tea Room at the Yasui Konpira-gu Shinto Shrine in Kyoto, Japan, and at the G.T.E. World Headquarters in Dallas, Texas. Begins to experiment with 'Niijima Floats' series working with gaffer Richard Royal.
1992	Creates major new architectural installations for traveling retrospective exhibition at the Seattle Art Museum, 'Dale Chihuly: Installations 1964-1992.' Recreates *20,000 Pounds of Ice* (1971) temporary installation for Seattle Art Museum, Honolulu Academy of Arts and the Contemporary Arts Center, Cincinnati, Ohio. Begins 'Chandeliers.' Large scale architectural installations commissioned for Little Caesar's Corporate Headquarters in Detroit and Corning Glass Headquarters in Corning, New York. Develops stage sets for 1993 Seattle Opera production of Claude Debussy's *Pelléas et Mélisande*. 'Pilchuck Stumps' grows out of these designs. Receives first National Living Treasure Award given in the United States.
1993	'Chihuly: Form from Fire' begins tour in U.S. 'Chihuly in Australia' opens at the Powerhouse Museum, Sydney.

Selected Museum Collections

Albright-Knox Art Gallery, Buffalo, New York
American Craft Museum, New York
American Glass Museum, Millville, New Jersey
Amon Carter Museum, Fort Worth, Texas
Arkansas Arts Center, Little Rock
Art Gallery of Greater Victoria, Victoria, British Columbia
Art Museum, Arizona State University, Tempe
Australian National Gallery, Canberra
Azabu Art and Crafts Museum of Tokyo, Japan
Boca Raton Museum of Art, Florida
Boston Museum of Fine Arts
Carnegie Museum of Art, Pittsburgh
Chrysler Museum, Norfolk, Virginia
Cleveland Art Museum, Ohio
Contemporary Arts Center, Cincinnati, Ohio
Contemporary Arts Center of Hawaii, Honolulu
Cooper-Hewitt Museum, The Smithsonian Institution National Museum of Design, New York
Corning Museum of Glass, New York
Crocker Art Museum, Sacramento, California
Currier Gallery of Art, Manchester, New Hampshire
Dallas Museum of Fine Arts, Dallas, Texas
De Cordova and Dana Museum and Park, Lincoln, Massachusetts
Denver Art Museum, Colorado
The Detroit Institute of Arts
Elvehjem Museum of Art, University of Wisconsin, Madison
Everson Museum of Art, Syracuse, New York
Fine Arts Museum of The South, Mobile, Alabama
Galerie d'art contemporain, Nice, France
Glasmuseum, Ebeltoft, Denmark
Glasmuseum Frauenau, Germany
Glasmuseum Wertheim, Germany
Haaretz Museum, Tel Aviv, Israel
High Museum of Art, Atlanta
Hokkaido Museum of Modern Art, Japan
Honolulu Academy of Art, Hawaii
Hunter Museum of Art, Chattanooga, Tennessee
Indianapolis Museum of Art, Indiana
Israel Museum, Jerusalem
Japan Institute of Arts and Crafts, Tokyo
Jesse Besser Museum, Alpena, Michigan
Kestner Museum, Hannover, Germany
Krannert Art Museum, University of Illinois, Champaign
Kunstindustrimuseum Kopenhagen, Denmark
Kunstmuseum, Dusseldorf, Germany
Kunstammlungen der Veste Coburg, Germany
Kyoto Museum, Japan
Leigh Yawkey Woodson Art Museum, Wausau, Wisconsin
Lobmeyr Museum, Vienna
Los Angeles County Museum of Art
Lowe Art Museum, Coral Gables, Florida

Lyman Allyn Art Museum, New London, Connecticut
Madison Art Center, Wisconsin
Metropolitan Museum of Art, New York
Milwaukee Art Museum, Wisconsin
Morris Museum, Morristown, New Jersey
Musée des Arts Décoratifs, Palais du Louvre, Paris
Musée des Arts Décoratifs, Lausanne, Switzerland
Musée des Beaux Arts et de la Ceramique, Rouen, France
Museum Bellerive, Zurich
Museum Boymans-Van Beuningen, Rotterdam, The Netherlands
Museum fur Kunst und Gewerbe, Hamburg, Germany
Museum fur Kunsthandwerk, Frankfurt, Germany
Museum of Art, Fort Lauderdale, Florida
Museum of Art, Rhode Island School of Design, Providence
Museum of Modern Art, New York
Museum of Contemporary Art, Chicago
Muzeum Mesta Brna, Brno, Czechoslovakia
Muzeum Skla A Bizuterie, Jablonec nad Nisou, Czechoslovakia
National Museum, Stockholm, Sweden
National Museum of American Art, Renwick Gallery, The Smithsonian Institution, Washington, D.C.
National Museum of Modern Art, Kyoto
New Orleans Museum of Art, Louisiana
Newport Harbor Art Museum, Newport Beach, California
Palm Beach Community College Art Museum, Florida
Parrish Museum of Art, Southampton, New York
Philadelphia Museum of Art, Pennsylvania
Phoenix Art Museum, Arizona
Portland Art Museum, Oregon
Princeton University Art Museum, New Jersey
Provincial Musée Sterckshof, Antwerp, Belgium
Queensland Art Gallery, Brisbane
Royal Ontario Museum, Toronto, Canada
Saint Louis Art Museum, Missouri
San Francisco Museum of Modern Art, California
Seattle Art Museum, Washington
Shimonoseki City Art Museum, Japan
J.B. Speed Art Museum, Louisville, Kentucky
Spencer Museum of Art, University of Kansas, Lawrence
Suomenlasimuseo, Riihimaki, Finland
Tacoma Art Museum, Washington
Toledo Museum of Art, Ohio
Umeleckoprumsylove Muzeum, Prague
Utah Museum of Fine Arts, Salt Lake City
Victoria and Albert Museum, London
Wadsworth Atheneum, Hartford, Connecticut
Walker Hill Art Center, Seoul
Whatcom Museum of History and Art, Bellingham, Washington
Whitney Museum of American Art, New York
Yale University Art Gallery, New Haven, Connecticut
Yokohama Museum, Japan

Chihuly's Vocabulary of Form

Since beginning to experiment with the material of glass in
the mid-1960s, Dale Chihuly has always worked in series.
He explores one aesthetic area and then moves on to
another, although he has never completely abandoned a
series. Occasionally there may be a break with a later
return to a theme, usually with increased scale and flam-
boyance. The development of Chihuly's oeuvre has been
marked by two kinds of changes, some subtle transitions,
as the transformation of the 'Baskets' into the 'Sea Forms,'
and others more radical as when he abruptly began the
exuberantly coloured 'Macchia.' Due to the size of this
exhibition, it was impossible to include examples of each
body of work, but this vocabulary of form describes the
basic series that have occupied Chihuly for nearly 20 years.

Cylinders 1974
Begun in 1974 as the 'Navajo Blanket Series.' Subsequently
more colourful, expressionistic, larger. Characterized by
surface decoration with 'glass pick-up drawings' primarily
of Native American textiles, recalling Chihuly's earlier
involvement with weaving. The 'Soft Cylinders' appeared
in 1986, the stolid earlier forms giving way to inflated and
collapsed shapes.

Baskets 1977
Inspired by seeing Northwest Coast Indian baskets piled
inside each other in the storerooms of the Washington State
Historical Society, an attempt to simulate the woven forms
that had sagged under their own weight. First time Chihuly
grouped vessels into sets. Originally earth-toned and red,
later turquoise, sunny yellow and white.

Sea Forms 1980
With the use of optic moulds to increase the strength of the
thin-walled glass and the shift in colour to whites, pinks and
grays, the 'Baskets' metamorphosed into the 'Sea Forms.'
Chihuly recalls that this was an unconscious process, but
immediately recognized the aesthetic potential. In many
ways representing the apogee of Venetian-style glass with
their delicacy.

Macchia 1981
Lusciously, even garishly coloured 'Macchia' replaced the
delicate 'Sea Forms' when Chihuly decided to use all 300
colours of glass commercially available. Distinguished by
multi-coloured spots and use of contrasting hues on interior
and exterior, separated by a layer of white chunks of glass
('clouds'). A lip wrap of yet another colour outlines the
opening of the vessel. Name Italian for 'spotted' or

'speckled' suggested by artist Italo Scanga. Also refers
to a mid-19th-century school of Italian painters, the
Macchiaioli, and the use of the word to mean 'sketchy'
and 'unfinished,' done in a Pointillist style.

Persians 1986
Exotic forms reminiscent of Middle Eastern vessels of the
12th- to 14th centuries. Surface decoration consists of
spiraling 'body wraps' and herringbone effects in a single
colour. On a large scale, frequently used for architectural
installations such as the *Venturi Window* done for the
Seattle Art Museum exhibition, 'Dale Chihuly: Installations
1964-1992.'

Venetians 1988
Inspired by Art Deco Venetian glass. Series begun with
Italian maestro Lino Tagliapietra. Developed further
by Chihuly's American team headed by Richard Royal.
In 1990 series expanded to include vessels with solid,
hot-worked glass *putti* created by Pino Signoretto from
Murano. Series has developed to include vessel forms with
attachments that refer to examples from decorative arts
history, such as prunts recalling Germanic glass of the
16th- to 17th centuries and flowers and vines reminiscent
of French Art Nouveau pieces.

Ikebana 1990
Variation of 'Venetians.' Title refers to Japanese art of
flower arranging. Glass flowers and stems in usually simple
gourd-like vessels. Suggested by request of Japanese
ikebana master to use Chihuly forms for his arrangements.

Niijima Floats 1991
Large spheres (up to 40 inches in diameter and 60 pounds).
Surfaces richly coloured and with gold and silver leaf and
foil. Named for Japanese fishing floats Chihuly found as a
child on the shores of Puget Sound and a small island in
Tokyo Bay with a glass school modeled on Pilchuck Glass
School, founded by Chihuly in 1971. (Not included in
exhibition.)

Pilchuck Stumps 1992
Mould-blown with iridescent surfaces, exploration of an
idea generated by sets Chihuly designed for the Seattle
Opera's production of Claude Debussy's *Pelléas et
Mélisande*. First time Chihuly has used the mould-blowing
technique. Each piece unique as mould is altered in the
process. (Not included in exhibition.)

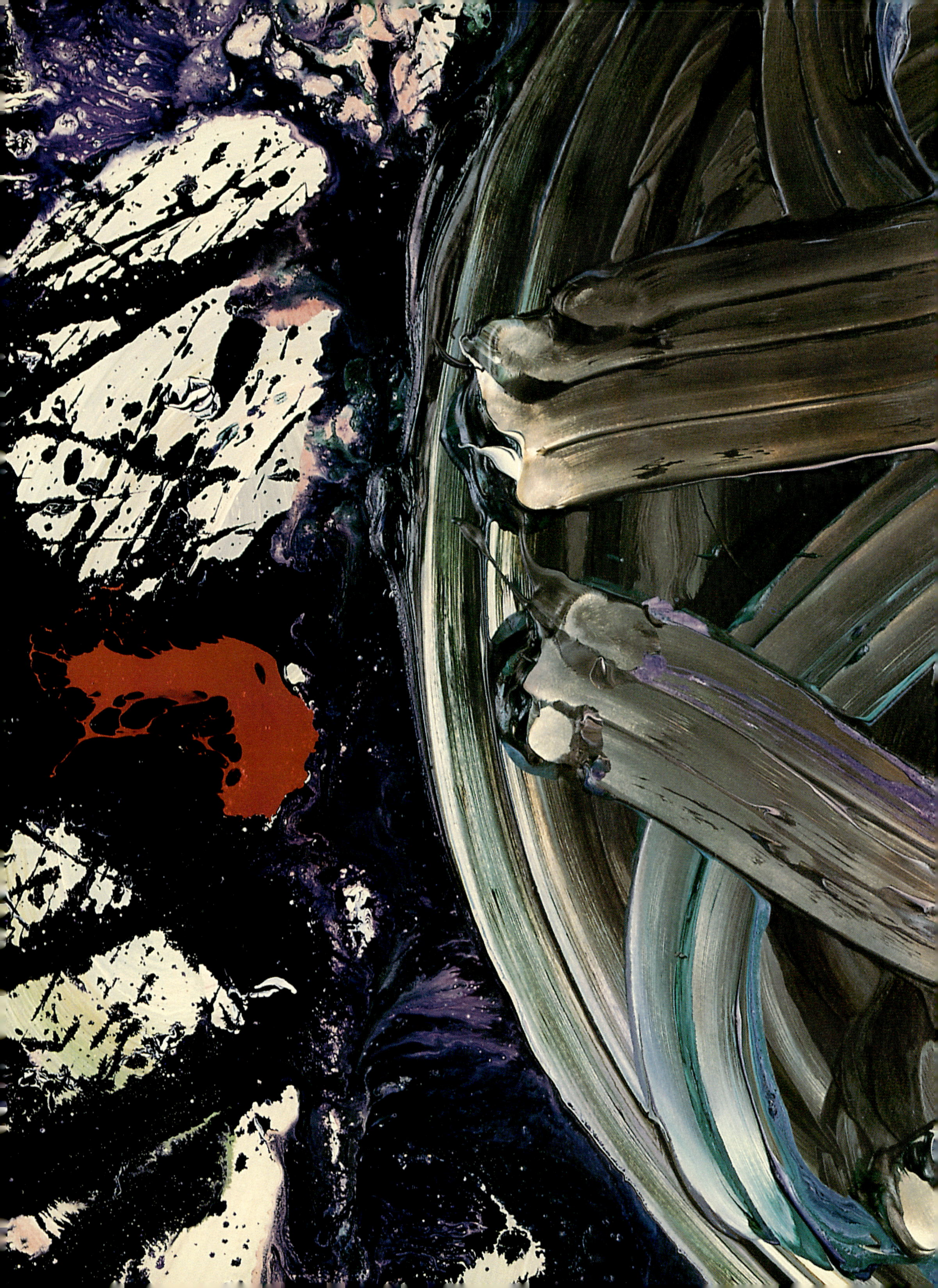